AF507413

About the Book

This book is written for self reflecting purposes. It is not people or things that hold us back, it is our thoughts about past events. For this book to be very effective, there are three requirements. The reader should be honest with self and dedicated. This book is filled with self reflective questions that will help you dig into yourself and understand yourself better. Sometimes we have to find our own way and this book helps you in doing that. Third requirement is a notepad and pen. Write down the answers to the questions given in each section. At the end an imagination exercise is given, kindly practice that.

Before you start have a particular past event in mind that you would like to get over. It is very effective if you can go through the whole book in one sitting. This is a direct to the point book. Different types of questions are asked by answering them you will get to know yourself better.

About the Author

I am Amal Prince, did my masters in literature and business, got into teaching field in 2007. After that I went on to do certain other courses related to life coaching. I have finished Cognitive Behavioural Therapy Coach Practitioner,Emotional Intelligence Practitioner,Rational Emotive Behaviour Therapy Practitioner,Emotional Intelligence Life Coach, Neuroscience of Reframing, Neuro Linguistic Programming Master Practitioner, Life purpose Coach Practitioner,Solution Based Counseling Practitioner, Diploma in Modern Applied Psychology, Strategic Life Coaching Practitioner.

I am also a member of CTAA-Complementary Therapists Accredited Association.

Content

Step I

1. How did this happen?

Even though it sounds like a silly question, look into the things that had to come together in order for this incident to happen. Write down each and everything that you feel had to come together for this incident to happen.

____

____

____

____

____

____

____

____

____

____

____

2. Why did this happen?

There will be a major reason why this has happened, What is that? What gave the opportunity for this to happen? Write down the things that you think gave opportunity for this incident to happen. When we look at event we always see what made this event possible, If you don't clearly see now, list out all the possibilities and start analyzing how it gave the opportunity.

What triggered this incident?

____

____

____

____

____

____

____

____

____

____

____

3. How did I contribute?

This is one question that you need to answer without having any kind of bias. When we believe that it is because of someone else we had a bad experience, we fail to see what part we played there. Discovering this will help us tremendously as it will show us whether we have this pattern in us. Take time to list out in detain your contribution to making this incident happen.

____

____

____

____

____

____

____

____

____

____

____

____

4. Was there a possibility to avoid this?

What has happened we cannot change but by answering this question we can actually see what we missed then. Was there a possibility to avoid this?

____

____

____

a. What could have avoided it?

____

____

____

b. What action from your part would have avoided this incident?

____

____

____

____

____

b. Was there anything that you could have done then to avoid that?

____

____

____

c. If yes –Why didn't you avoid it? Write down what you thought at that time. When we are face with situations we try to make the best choice possible. At that time what was the reason you had for not avoiding the incident? The answer to this question will help you understand yourself in a deeper level.

____

____

____

____

____

d. The reason you had for not avoiding it was it logical?

> After you answer the question, see where this same reason is playing a part in your current situation. If you see it write it down and see where your decisions are based on logic.

____

____

____

____

____

5. Now to be more clear – what were the early signs that you missed, which could have helped you in avoiding it?

____

____

____

____

Step II

1. Now looking back at that event do you feel that you have changed as a result of that incident?

____

____

____

____

____

2. How has this event changed you in a positive way?
   It might be difficult in the beginning to see any positive results from a hurtful incident. But if we look deep we can always see the positive effect it had on us.

____

____

____

____

____

3. What lessons did I learn from it?

Each and every time something happens to us
we tell ourselves something that we learnt
from it. What lessons did you learn
from it? Make a list

____

____

____

____

____

____

____

____

____

____

4. What else can be learnt from it?
   If we come to a negative conclusion as a
   lesson we learnt then it is negative thinking.
   We need to learn lessons that are positive in
   nature. What positive lessons did you
   learn and what else can be learnt?

____

____

____

____

____

____

____

5. What positive ability or character
   did you get or develop as a result of
   this incident?

____

____

____

6. What have you learnt that can help you avoid such events in the future?

Step III

1. Did this event affect you in a positive or negative way?

   Write down the things that you did as a result of this incident. Put them in two groups, positive and negative.

____

____

____

____

____

____

____

____

____

2. **What areas of your life were affected by it?**
   See the initial impact it had on your life and
   the other areas also got affected as a result of
   the initial impact. **Make a list**

   ____

   ____

   ____

   ____

   ____

   ____

   ____

3. **What beliefs and decisions did you
   make as a result of this event?**

   ____

   ____

   ____

____

____

____

____

4. What changes have happened to
   your life as a result of these beliefs
   and decisions?

____

____

____

____

____

____

____

5. The beliefs and decisions that
   originated as a result of the event,
   are they logical, true and Positive?

Take some time to answer this, as
what you find out can really make a
big difference.

____

____

____

____

____

____

____

6. If given a choice what positive
   beliefs and positive decisions can
   you make from this past incident?

____

____

____

____

____

Step IV

1. How did you view that incident till now? _______________________

____

____

Are you biased when you look back at it?_______________________

____

____

2. When you focused on this incident did it emotionally drain you?

____

____

____

3. Are you angry with yourself for what happened? _______________________
Have you forgiven yourself for what happened?_______________________

____

4. Did you have today's wisdom back then?___________________________

____

5. If you had today's wisdom back then, how different things would have been?___________________

____

6. As you didn't have today's wisdom back then can you blame yourself for what happened?_______________

____

____

7. What do you need to believe so that you can let go of this incident and the emotions attached to it?
See deep in yourself what belief can actually help you in letting it go.

____

____

____

____

____

____

____

____

8. What do you need to believe so that
   you can understand that this incident
   didn't break you but made you
   stronger?

____

____

____

____

____

____

____

____

Step V

1. In this past event did you behave or
   act according to the expectations
   others have/had for you?__________

   ____

   ____

2. What are the expectations others had
   for you?
   Separate them into two groups,
   positive and negative.

   ____

   ____

   ____

   ____

   ____

   ____

   ____

3. Why are these negative expectations about you not true?__________________

____

____

____

____

Write in details why those negative expectations are wrong.

____

____

____

____

____

____

____

____

____

4. What kind of positive character will
   show that those negative
   expectations are not true?

   ____

   ____

   ____

   ____

   ____

   ____

   ____

   ____

5. What other positive characters do
   you have?

   ____

   ____

   ____

   ____

   ____

Step VI

1. What advice will your well-wisher give you to help you let go of this incident?_______________

____

____

2. What will your best friend say to you, to support you and help you let go of it?_______________

____

____

3. What would your spiritual guide say to you?_______________________

____

____

4. What will your logical self tell you that can help you let go of it? ______

____

____

5. What advice would a good
   Samaritan stranger give you about
   the incident?_______________________

   ____

   ____

6. What does your higher successful
   version have to say?_________________

   ____

   ____

7. What would the independent version
   of yourself say?___________________

   ____

   ____

Step VII

1. What can you tell yourself to convince you to let go of this past incident?_______________________

____

____

2. What false emotional benefit were you getting by not letting it go?____

____

____

3. Why you no longer need that false emotional benefit?_______________

____

____

4. What other positive emotion can you use to replace this old false emotion?

____

____

____

5. As you are not your old (back then)
   version, isn't it time to let go of it?_

   ____

   ____

6. Isn't this incident a past event?
   Didn't it loose its effect over time?_

   ____

   ____

7. Isn't it time to move on?___________

   ____

8. Imagine this old event like a leaf in
   your hand. Look at it, as you are
   looking it is rapidly losing its color
   and becoming dark. The leaf is
   drying up very fast. Now it has
   become a dry leaf and feels very
   light. Imagine you are holding up
   your hands and this dried, brown
   leaf in your hands. A gentle breeze
   started to blow and suddenly the

breeze became stronger and lifted this leaf from your hands. You can see your dried, brown leaf flying away from you to a far far place. Suddenly you feel like a part of you is light and free. You turn around and feel that there is no more need to look back. You feel you are completely free.

Find a nice quiet place and sit or lie down, be completely relaxed. Take a deep breath and release slowly, do it three times. Close your eyes and start to imagine as given above. Let nothing disturb you while you do this.

Hope you enjoyed this book and found it useful. What motivates me the most is when readers write a review about the amazing transformation that happened through reading my book. If you truly feel that this book has helped you even in the slightest way kindly write a review.
                    Thank you
                    By Amal Prince